STAND
(Stand Take Authority Never Doubt)

STAND

(Stand Take Authority Never Doubt)

By
Dottie Shanks

Copyright © 2013 by Dottie Shanks

STAND
Take Authority Never Doubt
by Dottie Shanks

Printed in the United States of America

ISBN 9781625090041

All rights reserved solely by the author. The author guarantees all contents are original and do not infringe upon the legal rights of any other person or work. No part of this book may be reproduced in any form without the permission of the author. The views expressed in this book are not necessarily those of the publisher.

Unless otherwise indicated, Bible quotations are taken from The Scofield Reference Authorized King James Version of the Holy Bible. Copyright © 1909, 1917, Copyright renewed, 1937, 1945 by Oxford University Press Inc.

www.xulonpress.com

Dedication

I would like to dedicate this book to God, the real author, for without Him it would not have been possible. Also to Bishop Michael Torney and First Lady Joyce Torney, my spiritual father and mother in the Lord, who were responsible for instructing me in my walk with God. I received the Holy Spirit under their leadership. They have walked impeccably before me, and I love them dearly. To my beloved husband, Harvey G. Shanks; my son, Anthony G. Shanks; his wife, Diane Shanks; and Mother Fannie Torney, a true virtuous woman in the Lord, for displaying unshakable faith in teaching me about true holiness.

CONTENTS

Dedication vii
Foreword xi
Introduction xiii

Chapter One - What It Takes to Stand
       Faith 19

Chapter Two - Relationships
       Relationship with God 29
       Love 35

Chapter Three - Holiness
       What Is Holiness? 39
       Getting Rid of Your Junk 44
       Walking in the Shadow of God 47
       Making an Impact 50

Chapter Four - Recognizing the Devil and
Overcoming His Tactics
       How the Devil Operates 53
       False Doctrines 60
       If It's New Is It True? 63

Chapter Five – Conclusion: Victory
       You Have the Victory 71

Chapter Six - God's Word to Stand On 74

Foreword

We met Dottie through our cousin Harvey Shanks, her husband. We all were young members of the Bible Way Church World-Wide. Upon meeting Dottie I was an evangelist, and during one of my sermons she received God's Holy Spirit. Dottie has a tender heart for God and His Word and has always been eager to learn and grow. She is a sweet, honest, sincere person who has grown in God's knowledge, wisdom, and grace. She has a unique ministry in that God touches the hearts and changes the lives of everyone she comes in contact with. I can speak for the first lady in saying that we love Dottie with all our hearts.

May God continue to bless you in all that you do for His glory.

Bishop Michael Torney
South Toms River, New Jersey

Introduction

The Holy Spirit woke me up one night at 4:30 a.m. and compelled me to warn God's people to "listen to the Spirit." The still small voice said, "You don't have to write it; listen to Me and I will tell you what to write." I asked God, "But how can I explain this to those who don't know You, those who don't know about You and the Father being one?" He answered, "You tell your story and I will tell mine." The time has come and the hour is now when My people need to hear what I told them before, and he that hears and receives this will run, because it's going to be like fire shut up in their bones. It is written in the book of Revelation "He that hath an ear, let him hear what the Spirit saith unto the churches."

For those who know God you must listen to what the Spirit is saying to you. For those who have heard about Him and want to know Him, I encourage you to follow me as I tell you about my journey and what I heard in the Spirit. I hope you will listen, because you need to hear!

Many books have been written about God and Christianity, but none like this one. Why? This book is special because I have no claim to fame, nor am I a renowned author—just a regular person like many of you. But God has chosen me at this time to warn and remind His people again about the dangers which lie ahead and what they need to know in order to **stand**. This is an urgent call for God's people to listen and hear what He already told them before. Why? There is a time and a season for everything written in the Bible to manifest itself.

I believe God wants those who have decided to take a stand and walk with Him to inform everyone we can about what it takes to stand and why we are surviving, and to let them know He is still with them, His promises have not changed, we are still standing, and they can too. The Scripture says, "For God gave the word and great was the company that published it" (Psalm 68:11). This is that period in time when God said to tell His story to His people again; it will be a **refresher** of what they once knew because they have forgotten.

Today more than ever before people need to find a secure place to **stand**. The perilous times have arrived and life has become challenging, and we have to be equipped for this journey.

This book is a must read for ALL who have been sidetracked and lost your vision, hope, and purpose because you have been attacked by our adversary the devil. You see what's happening every day, and by the time 2013 ends you will be running to purchase this book. Why? It's time to **stand and take authority**.

Books have always been my passion. There is one book in particular which captured my heart: the Holy Bible, the inspiring Word of God. After being healed of a medical condition without surgery, I became a believer that God can operate without any tools; the scar is there, but I never had any surgery. Now I realize why God wants those who really believe in Him to tell their stories. God can take a nobody to tell everybody His story. I have been taking notes for years about the authority of Jesus, and now I know the purpose for taking them. God has been my guide and instructor in all things, and I feel chosen at this time to tell **His story again**.

One morning while writing this book I was overshadowed by the Holy Spirit. I explain this incredible experience in one of the following chapters; God is still visiting His people. I have been guided each step of the way in writing this book by a flicker of light which appeared at random times.

God does not care about your status in life, how educated you are, or how great you think you are. He said (Galatians 6:3), "For if a man think himself to be something, when he is nothing, he deceives himself." God is only concerned about your soul because He can use whoever, whatever, and whenever He wants to get His story told.

Introduction

As great as Abraham was, God said, "Before Abraham was I AM." He used a little rugged shepherd boy like David, who was herding and caring for sheep in the field, and Rahab the harlot to get His job done.

I have searched the Scriptures, embraced His truth, and accepted the challenge to stand and tell His story to all who will listen. I beseech you not to let this be another voice crying in the wildness trying to prepare and show His people the way, but I hope that someone will hear and remember their salvation. Luke 1:17 says, "And he shall go before him in the spirit and power of Elias, to turn the hearts of the fathers to the children, and the disobedient to the wisdom of the just; to make ready a people prepared for the Lord."

So I immediately sat down and began to write what I heard. This is to remind, inspire, and encourage those who have been hindered in their walk with God and need to take a stand to continue on their journey. It's for those who know Him and those who have heard about Him but don't know Him. The choice is yours, and the ones you make will determine your destiny. To make this journey you need hope, patience, and determination.

I heard in my spirit, "It is times like today, when you are reeling to and fro and are at wit's end, and it seems like everything is being shaken; you are facing so many struggles and challenges in your life, and the world looks like it has turned upside down; people are calling evil good and good evil, and you really don't know what to do; this is when you need to remember what Jesus said about seeking Him first." Matthew 6:33 says, "But seek ye first the kingdom of God, and his righteousness; and all these things shall be added unto you." But it's hard to find somewhere to stand if you don't remember what Jesus Word said about building upon the rock. It is written [Matthew 16:18], I say also unto thee, that thou art Peter, and upon this rock I will build **my church**; and the gates of hell shall not prevail against it. That is when you need to take that stand and remember your fortress. We are the **church**!

God is calling His people to continue to stand in these perilous times. He said, "Faithful is he that calleth you who also will do it" (1 Thessalonians 5:24). You have been chosen by God for such a time as this. Matthew 22:14 reads, "For **many are called**, but **few are**

chosen." Remember your instructions for this time in your life. It is written, "He would keep you in perfect peace whose mind is stayed on Him." You have to let God be your guide.

Do you remember what Jesus said?

> Therefore whosoever heareth these sayings of mine, and doeth them, will be a wise man, which built his house upon a rock, and when the rains, floods and the wind descended it did not fall, and to everyone that heareth these sayings of His, and doeth them not, shall be like the foolish man, who built his house upon the sand, and when the storms came it fell, because it was not firm enough to stand Matthew 7:24-25.

I remember my second week after I resigned from my job and I didn't know where to start. There were so many things to do, so many things I knew I should be doing, and my mind was racing so fast—*do this, do that!*—that I was overwhelmed. Then I remembered: what would Jesus do? I had not asked Him for help!

In the midst of the confusion I heard **STOP**. I am saying this to myself and to you also. Just stop! Get back into the Word of God to find out what to do. Stand, be still, and **listen to God**. We have to slow down because when you slow down you see things clearer. We are all busy people and we are always trying to sort out everything ourselves. We think we are in total control, but we are not—God is. Did you forget what He said? Without Him you can do nothing.

Just look at the environment we are living in today. Everything has become instant. Whatever we do must be quick, and society has provided every tool we need to do it, from email and Facebook to Twitter and YouTube. A click and you are on the air with thousands of people, telling your story. What about His story? Whatever we do it has to be quick. We need it right now! I heard the Spirit say, "If you are that busy, did you stop to ask Me for guidance?" Or do you still **remember Him**?

Have you been too busy to notice that when you go to the food store to buy your usual items, the names have changed? It used to be Quaker Oats, now it's Quick Quaker Oats, Quick Grits, Instant

Introduction

Oatmeal, Dinner in a Minute. And forget about the children; they are eating fast foods to keep up with their busy schedules. There are express windows at the banks and speed pumps at the gas stations. Some of the fast food places have created standup tables so you don't have to wait for a seat so they can serve you faster. And don't forget the self-serve counters so you don't have to wait in long lines. Whatever we do it has to be quick, quick, quick. If you are that busy, where is God's time?

I heard a voice that said we need to "be still, and know that I am God: I will be exalted among the heathen; I will be exalted in the earth" (Psalm 46:10). It is the same thing God has been saying from the beginning, when He spoke to Moses as he was leading the people out of the wildness according to God's instructions. "And Moses said unto the people, Fear ye not, stand still, and see the salvation of the LORD, which He will show to you today: for the Egyptians whom ye have seen today, ye shall see them again no more forever" (Exodus 14:13). Moses showed the people what happened because he wanted them to see that God could take care of their problem.

This is why we need to slow down. This is why we have days, weeks, months, and years to accomplish our goals. God did not create everything in one day!

Acknowledging God still works if you allow Him. God inspired me to **remind** and **inform** His people how to sustain themselves by renewing their minds on the instructions He left. Romans 12:2 says, "and be not conformed to this world, but be ye transformed by the renewing of your mind, that ye may prove what is that good, and acceptable, and perfect **will** of God."

Please read this book prayerfully because I know there is a blessing in here for you. Proverbs 28:20 says, "A faithful man shall abound with **blessings**: but he that maketh haste to be rich shall not be innocent." And 1 Thessalonians 3:8 proclaims, "For now we live, if ye stand fast in the Lord."

Your equipment to stand according to God's Word is found in this book, and you need to read on. When you finish reading this book and look back over your life and remember the situations you got yourself into, which were destroying your life, or that accident or sickness which almost took your life, and the condition of your life and family right now, you will know you have been blessed. He has been there all the time, and you will have a testimony.

I must continue on this journey because I know I could not have written this on my own, and I give God all the glory! I hope you will be renewed after reading this book and follow His voice to victory. It's not me speaking but what I heard in the Spirit from the Father through me. I beseech you to read it completely before you come to any conclusions regarding the contents. Pray, receive, believe, decree, and expect change. I am just a believer and receiver.

Chapter One

What It Takes to Stand

Faith

"Now faith is the substance of things hoped for, the evidence of things not seen."
(Hebrews 11:1)

Remember when you first came to Christ believing in faith? This was the first step in your spiritual journey. I'm talking to those who know Him, reminding you to take a walk back in time with me and think about that day you first believed and received Jesus Christ as your Savior. I remember that day vividly; there was great peace and joy. It was like being in another world. I felt new and walked differently. I held my head high and thought to myself, *I am somebody*. I did not know what happened, but it was an amazing experience I had never felt before and really could not explain. The peace I felt surpassed all understanding. I looked at things differently and loved everybody. I did not think negatively about anyone. I could not see it, but I knew something had changed inside of me.

When I picked up that cross and started to follow Him, something began to happen. The Bible says, "Take up your cross and follow me and I will make you fishers of men" (Matthew 4:19). Jesus was saying "Let Me guide you," but the choice is yours to make and you can choose whatever you want to be. I chose to follow

Jesus and walk by faith. Today, when I think back about that day, I can still feel God's Spirit moving in the core of my stomach. Sometimes you need to look back at that new direction God placed you in to see if you are still on track. Are you still excited about Christ? Have your feelings for Him changed? Do you feel the same way you did when you first received Him into your life? Are you walking by faith? Think about these questions, because this is what I heard in the Spirit. If you don't feel that way, you need to do a self-check to see if you have left your "first love."

There is a song I love to sing called "At the Cross." The lyrics are: "At the cross at the cross where I first saw the light and the burdens of my heart rolled away, it was there by faith I received my sight, and now I am happy all the day." These lyrics describe exactly what God's Spirit moving through me felt like. The joy was overwhelming, everything felt good, and I knew something had taken place. What it was I did not know. Remember, I was a babe in Christ, and I knew nothing about God's Spirit.

That is what faith in God will do for you. Faith is having confidence, trusting in God's Word, and believing what you cannot see. Hebrews 11:1 tells us, "Now faith is the substance of things hoped for, the evidence of things not seen." And Hebrews 11:6 says, "But without faith it is impossible to please him: for he that cometh to God must believe that he is, and that he is a rewarder of them that diligently seek him." It is also written that "faith cometh by hearing, and hearing by the word of God" (Romans 10:17).

You must continue to hear, receive, and believe the Word of God because "the word preached will not profit you if it's not mixed with faith" (Hebrews 4:2). The more you hear and apply the Word the more your faith in God increases and the stronger you grow. It's like a newborn baby; when it's first born it can only consume milk because it cannot digest meat. The same is true for the Word of God. You have to grow in faith by continuing to hear the Word and most of all applying what you hear. Hebrews 5:14 says, "But strong **meat** belongeth to them that are of full age, even those who by reason of use have their senses exercised to discern both good and evil." You have to get to know God.

In order to hear God's Word you need to stay connected to Him. You can hear the Word of God in many ways, from television, radio, and other sources, but the Bible says in Romans 10:14-15, "How can you call on who you have not believed? And how can you believe what you have not heard? And how can you hear without a preacher, and how can he preach except he be sent?

At some point in your life you probably purchased a Bible, and now it graces the center of your table for a showpiece. Did you know that during the time of the Old Testament Hebrew kings God's instruction to His people was lost in the house of God (2 Kings 22:8-13)?

It's like the Bible in the New Testament today—it is God's instructions for us to live by. However, we are no longer living under the law but by God's grace. But if you are not reading the Word how will you know what God said, or what God's purpose is for your life, and how you can become stronger.

You need to find that Bible wherever you placed it, dust it off, and read it so your faith can increase. The more you hear and the more you read about God, the more confidence you will have in His Word. **Faith** is your anchor and stronghold when things get mentally and physically challenging, when you are going through those difficult times and don't know what to do next. Or do you still remember?

We are on a spiritual journey with hope, and you will need God's Spirit to make this journey. If you have received God's Spirit, you have to stir it up again. In 2 Timothy 1:6 it says, "Wherefore I put thee in **remembrance** that thou stir up the gift of God, which is in thee by the putting on of my hands." You have to get excited about being in Christ—shake yourself. I had to learn that. Have you noticed the instructions on some bottles and cans that say "shake before using"? Like a bottle of salad dressing of oil and vinegar. Sometimes the good stuff is at the bottom, and you have to shake it so it can rise to the top and mix with the oil. God's Word and faith have to be mixed together in order for them to be effective in your life.

God said, "For unto us was the gospel preached, as well as unto them, but the word preached did not profit them, not being **mixed with faith** in them that heard it" (Hebrews 4:2). You have to remember God's Word just as you remember to shake that bottle of dressing. You should be praising Him right now!

God said in John 14:26, "But the Comforter, which is the Holy Ghost, whom the Father will send in my name, he shall teach you all things, and bring all things to your remembrance, whatsoever I have said unto you." Your job is to remember to apply it when you are confronted. Stop and ask yourself, what did Jesus say about this situation, or what would He do? If you have fallen away renew your citizenship to the kingdom of God. Remember what you told Him when you first received His Spirit and became born again. Let's do the first works over. The Word of God promises that He will guide you continually because He is the "repairer of the breach, the restorer of paths to dwell in" (Isaiah 58:12). He is your foundation.

For all who have heard about God and don't know Him let me introduce Him to you. His name is Jesus, the name that is above every name. He is the Alpha and Omega, the beginning and the end, the Almighty God, the great I AM. He is the creator of all things and He is a Spirit (John 1: 3). When you receive God you get the Father, Son, and Holy Spirit—He performs all three roles. He is the Father in creation, the Son in redemption, and the Holy Spirit that indwells you all in one. It is written in John 10:30, "I and my **Father** are one, and if you have seen the Father you have seen me." It's the same as being a wife, a mother, and a grandmother. It depends on the role you are performing at the time. You are one person performing three different roles, and each role is different.

Acts 2:38 says, "Repent, and be baptized in the name of Jesus Christ for the remissions of sins, and ye shall receive the gift of the Holy Ghost, which is his Spirit." You can take that stand right now and repent of all your sins; ask Jesus to come into your life and take control because you cannot handle it anymore. Be sincere, mean what you say, and believe in Him. Be baptized in His name and receive the gift of the Holy Spirit. John 1:12 says, "But as many as received him, to them gave he power to become the sons of God, even to them that believed on his name." The Bible clearly reminds us in John 14:6 that "[He] is the way, the truth, and the life: no man cometh unto the father, but by me." There is no other way to enter in.

Romans 6:4 tells us, "We are buried with him by baptism into death, and like Christ was raised up from the dead by the glory of the Father, even so we also should walk in newness of life."

In John 3 Jesus answers the question from Nicodemus, a ruler of the Jews who came in secret to Jesus by night to see how he could enter the kingdom of God and be born again. Jesus said unto him, "Verily, verily, I say unto thee, except a man be born again, he cannot see the kingdom of God" (John 3:1). You don't have to come in secret to receive God's Spirit to enter the kingdom and reap His benefits. Jesus has already invited you to come. He said in Matthew 6:33, "But seek ye first the kingdom of God, and his righteousness, and all these things shall be added unto you." All you have to do is seek Him and the door will open.

Jesus knows we all have sinned. In Romans 3:23 it is written, "All have sinned and come short of the glory of God." Remember He made you and knows everything about you, and because you will be in Christ, there will be "no more condemnation to you, because you will be walking in Christ Jesus and not walking after the flesh, but after the spirit" (Romans 8:1). It does not matter what anyone else says about you, because you only have to please Him.

You can become that new creature Jesus is talking about in 2 Corinthians 5:17, which says, "Therefore if any man be in Christ, he is a new creature, old things are passed away; behold, all things are become new." He is talking about you.

After you receive Jesus Christ as your Lord and Savior you have to walk in Him, become rooted and built up in Him. Establish yourself in the faith. As the Bible says, you have to "put on the new man, which is renewed in knowledge after the image of God who has created you" (Colossians 3:10). Stand firm in Christ; be not moved about. Put down some roots. You don't want to be like a potted plant that can be moved from place to place, but like the tree planted by the rivers of water with deep roots, one that can "stand and still yield fruit when the heat or drought season comes" (Jeremiah 17:8).
Learn how to stand!

Walk worthy of the kingdom and your new citizenship. Your Father is the King. If you are stuck in a rut, take a stand and think about the new direction you have taken. Romans 6:1-4 says, "What shall we say then? Shall we continue in sin, that grace may abound? God forbid." God wants His people to walk worthy of their callings. Romans 6:14 tells us "sin shall not have dominion over you, for ye are not under the law, but under grace." And God says "His grace is sufficient for you" (2 Corinthians 12:9).

When you start out in Christ the devil knows, and he will launch all kinds of attacks to hinder you. Keep your eyes and mind on Christ. There is a warning from God which says, "No man having put his hand to the plow, and looking back is fit for the kingdom of God" (Luke 9:62). Stay focused. Keep looking to Jesus for everything; He is your source and the author and finisher of your faith (Hebrews 12:2). The Word says, "He will keep you in perfect peace whose mind is stayed on thee, because you have trusted in Him" (Isaiah 26:3).

I have been discouraged many times during my walk with God. There have been times when it was good, times when it was bad, and times when it was unbearable, but I am **still standing**, hallelujah. I realize that this will be a long journey, and I have no idea what lies ahead. But God is faithful and has not put more on me than I can bear. Yes, I have lost some things and failed some tests, and probably will fail some more, but now I have grown in faith and remember what the Word says about the situations. "My grace is sufficient for you, and if you faint in the day of adversity, your strength is small" (Proverbs 24:10).

Cleave to the Word. James 4:8 says, "Draw nigh to God, and he will draw nigh to you." Be steadfast in the Word. Most of us want the rewards of the closeness with God without the consecration required to be close to Him. You have to submit yourself to God. Resist the devil. Cleanse your hands and purify your hearts to remain true to God. Remember that God is your leader and the Holy Spirit is your keeper. The Bible tells us, "For every way that you would be tempted, He has made a way for you to escape" (1 Corinthians 10:13). He knew you would be tempted because He was too (Hebrews 4:15). Look for that open door. There is an open door which God Himself has opened for you that no man can shut, because you have not denied His name (Revelation 3:8).

What It Takes To Stand

It takes a determined mind to serve Christ. When you get weary, and when unexpected circumstances come upon you and try your last measure of faith, that is when you must remember what Jesus said in Matthew 17:20 "If you have faith as a grain of mustard seed, ye shall be able to speak to that mountain [that situation] and it shall be moved, and nothing shall be impossible for you." Just believe and have faith in God! The Bible says, "Be not weary in well doing, because you will reap in due season, if you faint not" (Galatians 6:9).

Remember our afflictions are just for a while. Psalm 34:19 says, "Many are the **afflictions** of the righteous, but the LORD delivereth him out of them all." We "walk by faith and not by sight" (2 Corinthians 5:7). Regardless of what it looks like, stand on God's Word and call those things that be not as though they were.

This is why you have to remember what God said: "Cast not away your confidence, which hath great recompense of reward" (Hebrews 10:35), which means if you wait a little while it will come to pass. His Word has never changed since He spoke it. Abraham had that kind of faith in God. When God told Abraham (Genesis 22:2) to offer his only son Isaac as a sacrifice, he obeyed the Lord not knowing that God had already prepared a ram in the bush, because he could not see it. But Abraham was strong in his faith and believed God; he staggered not at the promise and took Him at His word.

In Matthew 14:28-30 when Jesus summoned Peter to come to Him, Peter walked on the water and prevailed as long as he kept his focus on Jesus, but the moment he took his mind off God and looked at the situation he failed. God said He would keep you in perfect peace whose mind is stayed on Him. He will not fail you. It is written in His Word; He will never leave you nor forsake you.

You have to develop more faith in God's Word. Be unmovable and unshakable when it comes to the Word, knowing that your faith is not in vain because God is able to do what He says He will do. Ephesians 3:20-21 says, "Now unto him that is able to do exceeding abundantly above all that we ask or think, according to the power that worketh in us, and unto him be glory in the church by Christ Jesus throughout all ages, world without end." Amen.

God said, "So shall my word be that goeth forth out of my mouth, it shall not return unto me void, but it shall accomplish that which I please, and it shall prosper in the thing whereto I sent it" (Isaiah 55:11). Do you still believe that?

Remember you are walking in the Spirit and not in the flesh. "For no man can serve two masters, for either he will hate the one, and love the other, or else he will hold to the one, and despise the other" (Matthew 6:24). And James 1:7-8 tells us, "A double minded man is unstable in all his ways." Who are you listening to?

You will have to let go of some things that hinder you. It could be people, habits, your attitude, relationships, or excess debt—all can create major disorder in your life. During this time, I guarantee you will take a stand and continue in that new direction God has chosen for you.

Regardless of the situation remain true in opposition; you have to stand and take authority and never doubt. Study the Word, apply the Word, and live the Word. Be doers of the Word and not hearers only. And, yes, you will have to get out of your comfort zone and do what God is telling you to do.

I remember I was looking for a job, and I followed what I heard and did what the Scripture said to do because I was learning to walk by faith and not by sight, and it worked. When I arrived there the devil also was there. I knew it was just a test. I did what the Bible said. I used the Word of God and took a stand and went to work. Standing on what I believed, I did not move until I heard God say "now it's time to go" because He had something else for me to do. I have learned to listen to God for my instructions before I proceed. You cannot hurry God. He has a time for everything, and I have also learned He is a very present help in time of trouble.

I am still being tested and you will be tested too. I have to remind myself always of who's going through the test with me, and I know in the end I will win. Yes, there have been times when I really had no answer and did not know what to do. During those times I remember to stay in the Word and the truth. Steadfastness tests your character. When you feel the weight of your problem, remember that "our light afflictions are but for a moment" (2 Corinthians 4:17).

Don't depart from the truth. If there was not a possibility to fall the Bible would not have said it's possible to fall from our steadfastness. Hebrews 4:11 says, "Let us labor therefore to enter into that rest, lest any man fall after the same example of unbelief." You have to know that, and Proverbs 16:25 reminds us, "There is a way which seemed right unto a man, but the end there of are the ways of death."

Stand and stay focused and continue to look to Jesus. After you have learned how to be obedient to Christ your job is to help others find their way. We are our brothers' keepers. You have to share what you know with others or you will be held accountable. If they read the Bible and don't understand what it means, explain it to them. Salvation is not just doctrine believed, but doctrine shared.

A story in Acts 8:26-39 really blessed my soul and touched by heart. It's about an angel of the Lord speaking to Philip and instructing him to go south toward Jerusalem into Gaza, which was a desert. Philip did not know why he was asked to go, but out of obedience he went. On the road he met a man of Ethiopia, a eunuch of great authority under the supervision of the Ethiopian queen who had come to Jerusalem to worship. He was in charge of all her treasure. Sounds like a very powerful man wouldn't you say.

The eunuch was sitting in his chariot reading Esaias the prophet, and Philip heard the Spirit say go near and join yourself to his chariot. He did not know why, but he ran to the chariot. **Notice I said he ran**. When he got there he heard the eunuch reading, and he asked him if he understood what he was reading. The eunuch answered, how can I, except some man should guide me? He asked Philip to come and sit with him. The eunuch was reading the Scripture verse "he was led as a sheep to the slaughter; and like a lamb dumb before his shearer, so opened he not his mouth: in his humiliation his judgment was taken away: and who shall declare his generation? for his life is taken from the earth."

The eunuch was puzzled and asked Philip who was the prophet speaking to, himself or some other man? Then Philip began to preach Jesus to him; and they continued on their journey. After a while they came unto certain water; and the eunuch asked to be baptized, because he believed what had been explained to him that Jesus Christ was the Son of God.

Philip commanded the chariot to stand still: and they went down into the water and he baptized the eunuch. When they came out of the water, the Spirit of the Lord caught away Philip and the eunuch saw him no more, but he went on his way rejoicing. Why? Because it had been explained to him what he had read and did not understand about the salvation plan.

This is a charge for all of us to tell all who have heard and read God's Word and still don't understand. Take the time to revisit Acts 8:26-39. You will be blessed!

Remember, you *are* your brother's keeper. "For unto whomsoever much is given, of him shall be much required" (Luke 12:48).

When you start out in Christ draw close to Him, study and apply the Word; God will keep you. Stand and take authority, never doubt. Remain true to God. It is written in the Word, "Not by power nor by might, but by his Spirit saith the Lord" (Zachariah 4:6).

God said in Deuteronomy 30:12,14: "His word is not in heaven, that thou shouldest say, who shall go up for us to heaven, and bring it unto us, that we may hear it, and do it? . . . But the word is very nigh unto thee, in thy mouth, and in thy heart, that thou mayest do it." And God repeated it again in Romans 10:8, which reads, "But what saith it? The word is nigh thee, even in thy mouth, and in thy heart: that is, the word of faith, which we preach." He was letting us know it was the same Word He had told them in the Old Testament, and it is still the same today. This is why you have to remember God's Word, so you will not sin against Him. Hide His Word in your heart and He will fight your battles.

God wants you to remember that "the name of the LORD is a strong tower, the righteous runneth into it, and is safe" (Proverbs 18:10). God is our refuge and strength, and we are made partakers of Christ "if we hold the beginning of our confidence steadfast unto the end" (Hebrews 3:14). You have to be confident in knowing that "He who hath begun a good work in you will perform it until the day of Jesus Christ" (Philippians 1:6).

Because you know His name He will not let you down. God said in Psalm 9:10, "And they that know thy name will put their trust in thee: for thou, LORD, hast not forsaken them that seek thee."

Chapter Two

Relationships

Relationship with God

"It is written in the prophets, and they shall be all taught of God. Every man therefore that hath heard, and hath learned of the Father, cometh unto me."
(John 6:45)

As you already know by now there are many kinds of relationships. Some are for a minute and some are in it to win it. This is a reminder to those who started a relationship with Jesus Christ. The two kinds of relationships I am talking about will determine what and how you should be building on them. They are different but have some of the same characteristics. The difference: one is natural and the other is spiritual. We need to remember that so they will not be misunderstood. The relationship you have with God is a special kind of relationship. It's a personal relationship between you and Him. You will not find the word *relationship* in the entire Bible because a relationship with God is by faith, believing in His name, receiving His Spirit, and being led by the Spirit to learn about Him.

The relationship you have with your spouse or friend is not the one you will have with God because that relationship is natural, fleshly, but the one you have with God is spiritual. You can see your spouse or friend and touch them and talk directly to them because they are in the flesh, but God is a Spirit and you need His Spirit to reach Him. That is why the Bible says in John 4:24, "God is a Spirit, and they that worship him must worship him in Spirit and in truth." This is why you have to be born again.

It is essential to get baptized in the name of Jesus and receive His Spirit and be born again. When you take on the name of Jesus and become a part of His kingdom, you are adopted into His spiritual realm, and the way you communicate with Him is through His Spirit because you cannot see Him. By being a part of that kingdom you are an heir and have the authority to use His name and many other benefits associated with it.

Think about this: have you communicated with God lately? Not to ask for something you want but to give Him the glory because you love Him?

How well do you know God? The Lord Himself prayed in John 17:3 "that we may know Him." In order to do this you have to submit to God, because it is from Him that we obtain the knowledge to have a personal relationship. Jeremiah 9:23 says, "Let not the mighty man glory in his might, nor let the rich man glory in his riches; but let him who glories glory in this, that he understands and knows me." You have to get to know Jesus just like you know your friend or spouse.

Page after page the Bible refers to getting to know God. "Take my yoke upon you and learn of me" (Matthew 11:29). "In all thy ways acknowledge him" (Proverbs 3:6). "Whosoever abideth in him sinneth not: whosoever sinneth hath not seen him neither known Him." It continues, "They profess that they know God; but in their works they deny him, being abominable, and disobedient, and unto every good work reprobate" (Titus 1:16). You have to get to know God and develop a personal relationship with Him and recognize His voice. John 10:27 says, "My sheep hear my voice, and I know them, and they follow me." Do you know why God said to get to know Him so many times? He is trying to develop a relationship with you.

Relationships are developed by getting to know a person. When I first met my husband I only knew his name, and over time we became friends. The longer we stayed together the closer we became, and a friendship developed. We found out we had some of the same mutual interests. We began to talk about things openly and became comfortable and gained respect for each other. It was more than knowing just his name and nothing else about him. And it was not an overnight journey. Today we are still learning things about each other. Is it easy? No, it requires a **LOT** of work. Sometimes there is pain and sometimes there is gain, but through each season we are still learning things about each other.

What we have learned is to forgive and forget, to give and take, and to keep going by building on what it took for us to get this far with our marriage. It is called LOVE. Remember "it covers a multitude of sins." And after forty-six years we are still standing! In 1 Peter 4:8 it says "and above all things have fervent charity among yourselves, for charity shall cover a multitude of sins." It's like what Jesus was saying in Matthew 11:29: "Take my **yoke** upon you, and learn of me; for I am meek and lowly in heart: and ye shall find rest unto your souls." This simply means to read your Bible, which is God's way of communicating with you. Get to know Him.

When you read the Bible, God reveals Himself to you. You don't have to see Him because He works through our hearts and minds, and when you are open with Him He becomes your spiritual light. He will open up His understanding to all who are interested in knowing the truth. If you don't believe Him it's because "the God of this world has blinded the eyes of them that believe not" (2 Corinthians 4:3-4). You have to recognize Him for who He is, make Him your focus in life, and learn to depend on and most of all obey and trust His Word. You may not always like what you hear. Sometimes He will chastise you, sometimes you will feel like He is not listening, and sometimes you may not hear anything at all, but stand anyhow because 1 Corinthians 2:5 says "your faith should not stand in the wisdom of men, but in the power of God."

All God asks of you is to have a place in your heart to receive Him, an open mind to listen to what the Spirit is saying to you, and to obey His Word. Obedience is better than sacrifice. Hebrews 3:7-8 says, "Today when you hear my voice harden not your hearts as in rebellion." From the day I first became born again, I have always loved Psalm 139:1-3, which reads, "Lord thou has searched me, and known me. Thou knowest my down sitting and mine uprising, thou understandest my thought afar off, and thou compassest my path and my lying down, and are acquainted with all my ways." Sometimes when I think back to the time when I did not know Him, I really feel blessed because I don't know what I would have done without God's guidance.

God is looking for a commitment from you. And you have to establish an agreement with Him. Amos 3:3 reads, "Can two walk together, except they be agreed?" You have to accept and believe what Jesus is saying to you or you will not be able to develop a relationship with Him. And, yes, God has some requirements for developing a relationship with Him.

He knows everything about you already, because Jeremiah 1:5 declares, "He knew you before you were formed in your mother's belly." He knows what you will and will not do. You can dye your hair and make all the cosmetic changes you want, even move to the other side of town, but He still knows who you are and where you are because He is omniscient. Remember He gave you that hair and numbered the strands on your head. Isn't that awesome! I have heard people say when you get to heaven God will not recognize you because of the things you have done to yourself. I have news for them; God will recognize you because He did not throw away the original blueprint of you. An original cannot be replaced. You can only make a copy. Only God has the original. Do you feel a shout coming on!

You have to fear Him. That does not mean you are scared of Him, because perfect love casts out all fear. Just take His Word seriously as Proverbs 1:7 says, "The fear of the LORD is the beginning of knowledge and understanding, but fools despise wisdom and instruction." Psalm 34:7-9 says, "The angel of the Lord encamped round about them that fear him." When you learn to obey Him that shows you are growing in the Lord. You will become closer to Him, and your relationship will begin to develop. You will depend on and

Relationships

trust Him more and follow His instructions. Proverbs 3:7 says, "Be not wise in thine own eyes: fear the LORD, and depart from evil."

I will tell you about two encounters I had with God—one happened before I knew Him and the other after I was born again, in fact very recently while writing this book.

The first encounter came during a time in our life when everything was going wrong in our home. We were at wit's end. This particular night the house had caught on fire. We were inside and could not see what was happening outside and did not know until our neighbor came over and told us the roof was on fire. I sought the Lord that night, and I remember saying I could not take this anymore. I remember the day vividly because I had a strange encounter that night.

As I watched an extremely bright light beam parted the curtains of my bedroom. The light was so bright it lit up the whole room. Yes, I was scared because I was not born again and did not know what the light was. The beam of light pointed straight up, and at the top I saw a beautiful city. It was so bright I had to shield my eyes to peek at it; I could not look at it directly. But there was a problem: I saw people on that beam of light struggling to get to the top where the light was, and I was at the bottom looking up—and then the light disappeared.

The next day was a Sunday, and when I went to church I accepted Jesus and received that light the same day. Nothing has been the same since. On Sunday, March 25, 1984, at 11 a.m. I became born again. Today I still look to that light for my guidance and hope. And I pray that I will always be led by that light. Every day I start the day by asking God for guidance, vision, courage, and strength, and I consecrate myself to Him by meditating on His Word during the day. What a difference it makes when you start your day with God.

I can stand here today and tell you it's important to stay in that light. You have to keep believing and have hope. The Word says in 1 John 3:3, "And every man that hath this hope in him purifieth himself, even as he is pure." You have to want and expect a change in your life.

No, I have not made it yet, but I learned you have to constantly remind yourself of how you made it this far and what it took to get here and what it is going to take to stand. You have to humble yourself, get to know God, submit to Him, obey Him, listen to Him, and apply His Word. Then you can stand and follow His instructions. He said in Psalm 46:10, "Be still, and know that I am God: I will be exalted among the heathen; I will be exalted in the earth."

You have to talk to God, develop a prayer life, so you will be able to recognize His voice. Listen and follow His instructions. The Word says, "In all thy ways acknowledge him, and he shall direct thy paths" (Proverbs 3:6). He will guide you if you ask Him.

My second encounter with God happened during the writing of this book. I did not write this book alone. I was guided each step of the way by a voice I heard late at night or early in the morning, usually around 5 or 6 a.m. and around midnight or 1:30 in the morning. I would get up and take notes on my iPhone so I could add them the next morning in the book. I used to sit for hours without getting up because the words came so fast and I was trying to type as fast as I heard what was being said.

One morning I was just getting started for the day when I was overshadowed by a presence I could not see. I was stumbling around, and I started to praise God and could not stop. I was shaking and crying and praising God, saying "thank You, Lord, I praise You, Lord, to God be the glory," and it did not stop.

I called my husband because I did not know what was going on—this had never happened to me before. I was totally overshadowed. He told me it was the glory of God and to let Him have His way. The praise finally stopped, but the feeling lasted all day.

When my husband got home from work I tried to tell him what had happened in detail. How I was standing in our home and everything looked different. The whole house had such a peace and calm presence I did not know what to think. I was there, but my body felt like it was lifted to another level; I really was somewhere else. It was overwhelming, and I began to cry and shake again as I explained it to him.

Take the time and get to know God, because He is real. And He will lead and guide you in everything you do if you allow Him.

Jesus said, "My sheep know my voice" (John 10:4-5). Get to know your Shepherd because He is watching over your soul. In the beginning when God created the first man Adam and breathed into his nostrils, and he became the first living soul, God had a purpose for creating him that way, so that He could communicate with Adam and know his feelings and his moral nature.

When your soul is alive it can praise God. Psalm 119:175 declares, "Let my soul live and it shall praise thee and let thy judgments help me." And Peter reminds us in 1 Peter 4:19, "Wherefore let them that suffer according to the will of God commit the keeping of their souls to Him in well doing, as unto a faithful Creator." You should "love God with all your heart and soul." James 1:21 says, "Wherefore lay apart all filthiness and superfluity of naughtiness, and receive with meekness the engrafted Word, which is able to save your soul." Develop that relationship with God and obey His Word so you will know what is required of you.

Whatever you do, keep your relationship with God truthful, faithful, and real.

Love

"By this shall all men know that ye are my disciples, if ye have love one to another."
(John 13:35)

Do you remember what love is and why you should love? If you are born again, you love because it's required of God. Why, because He is love. You cannot please Him if you do not possess this attribute. If you ask how you can love Him, your reminder is 1 John 4:19, which reads, "We love him, because he first loved us."

I will tell you about three kinds of love. Please read this with an open mind. They are eros, philos, and agape. In brief, **eros** is a strong feeling or impulse towards another; it's physical love. It is considered love at first sight, untested or emotional love. Then there is **philos,** which is mental or brotherly love that develops between two people and leads to friendship or a relationship. Philos takes time to build; it requires giving and taking. Finally, there is **agape** or unconditional love.

Agape love is "the kind of love God has for us," and it's above all the others. It's **spiritual**, the kind of love all of God's people must possess. It's the kind of love that makes you leave the things which do not please God and cleave to Him even though you cannot see Him, because He is a Spirit. The Bible says in 1 John 4:12, "no man hath seen God at any time." But "if we "love one another, God dwelleth in us, and his love is perfected in us." And "hereby know we that we dwell in him, and he in us, because he hath given us of his Spirit" (v.13). This is the kind of love you must have for God: giving without expecting to get anything in return.

And we are partakers of that Spirit, because God's children are born of Him. This is the kind of love in which a person will lay down his life for another person. The kind of love God has for us. He loved us so much He sent His only begotten Son into the world, and He became the sacrifice that we might live. He dwells in us, and His love is divine and is perfected in us. How could you not love a God like that? That's the kind of love I am talking about. It is the God kind of love. He said, "If you love me keep my commandments."

And by keeping His commandments we know Him, and if you say you know Him and keepeth not His commandments you are a liar and the truth is not in you. But if you keep His Word the love of God is perfected and we know that we are in Him. God wrote no new commandment, but the old commandment which you have heard from the beginning, which is the Word. You have to love everyone because you are now in the light and not darkness (1 John 2:3-5). Remember, God said, "Love worketh no ill to his neighbor, because it was the fulfilling of the law" (Romans 13:10). Yes, we are living by His grace, but it's still part of His commandment from the beginning—it has never changed. Love is love!

Read what God said in Deuteronomy 8:11-18: "Beware and forget not, but keep His commandments, judgments and statutes which He commanded you this day, because you have become good in your own eyesight and have become so plentiful that you have forgotten how you received it, and who set you free from bondage, who humbled you, that He might prove you in the end, because it's not your own might and power which has gotten you wealth. All your substance comes from the LORD."

Relationships

We have to love our brothers and sisters, including those who don't like us and those who lie to us or make promises and don't keep them. Why, because we are fulfilling the Word of God. If you say you love God and hate your brother or sister whom you see, how can you love God whom you cannot see? We have to overcome the things in the world by letting His Spirit rule our lives and keep us doing what His Word says to do. God is not a man that he should lie. By the Word you are condemned and by the Word you are justified. Love for God means overcoming the things in this world. Let us not love in tongue only but in deed and truth. If our hearts condemn us not then we have confidence towards God.

We have to love Him because God said so in His Word (1 John 4:7): "Beloved let us love one another; for love is of God and everyone that loveth is born of God and knoweth God. He that loveth not knoweth not God for he is love." We are His children and He is our Father, and we have to follow His instructions for our life. He laid down His life that we might have life.

Being a believer in union with Christ means doing what He did. Yes, sometimes it hurts, but if you suffer for the love of Christ there is much gain. And after a while you will be **able to stand**, because His commandments are not grievous (1 John 5:3).

We are instructed to guard our conversations and speak kindly to others always, because Colossians 4:6 says, "Let your speech be always with grace, seasoned with salt, that ye may know how ye ought to answer every man." Don't let your speech lose its savor; show others there is another way to approach whatever is taking place. When you confess that you are a child of God the devil starts to work on you, and that is when you have to remember that love covers a multitude of sins. Guard your mouth and keep your soul. Remember what God's Word said: "Evil communication corrupts good manners" (1 Corinthians 15:33). Ask God to help you not to speak evil against anyone.

Your hope is inside of you, and after you have done the will of God it will be well, because the Bible says, "He that has this hope purifieth himself even as he is pure" (1 John 3:3).

Walk humbly before the Lord because He has already told us how we should walk. His requirements are written. Micah 6:8 says,

"He hath shewed thee, O man, what is good and what he requires of you to be just and love mercy."

Abide in this love, because if you abideth in Him you ought to walk as He walked (1 John 2:6). Do it from your heart, in righteousness. You have to ask yourself daily what or how would God handle this situation, and remember what kind of character you are building. Is this like God? Talk to Him; He is listening. He never slumbers nor sleeps (Psalm 121:4).

I always go back and do self-checks to see if I am lining up with what the Word says about this love situation, because our gifts have to be governed by love. We want to be able to edify, exhort, clarify, and bring comfort to those we are speaking to.

In 1 Corinthians 13:13 a reminder is left about love. It reads, "And now abideth faith, hope, charity, these three, but the greatest of these is charity [love]." "And if you do this all men will know that you are my disciples" (John 13:35). We are followers of Christ. God is our Father and we are His children, so we should have some of His characteristics. Love does not destroy. You have to love like the Father has loved you and continue in it. The more you do it the easier it becomes. Jesus gave us a command in John 15:17. He said, "These things I command you, that ye **love** one another."

Chapter Three

Holiness

What Is Holiness?

"Follow peace with all men, and holiness, without which no man shall see the Lord."
(Hebrews 12:14)

Holiness is a way of life and is required of you. Why? Because the Word of God says, "But as he which hath called you is holy, so be ye holy in all manner of conversation, and be ye holy for I am holy" (2 Peter 1:15-16). Sanctification is a word you don't hear used very much anymore. It means clean or set aside, dedicated to God for a special purpose, pure—all of which is done by the cleansing of God's Word. In 2 Timothy 2:21 we read, "If a man therefore purge himself from these, he shall be a vessel unto honor, **sanctified**, and meet for the master's use, prepared unto every good work." Jesus let us know that "for their sakes I sanctify myself, that they also might be sanctified through the truth" (John 17:19).

From the beginning God has called for a holy people. In Deuteronomy 14:2 it is written, "For thou art an holy people unto the LORD thy God, and the LORD hath chosen thee to be a **peculiar** people unto himself, above all the nations that are upon the earth." And in 1 Peter 4:9 the Bible tells us, "Ye are a chosen generation, a royal priesthood, a holy nation, a **peculiar** people; that ye should shew forth the praises of him who hath called you out of darkness into his marvelous light." We are those peculiar people whom God has chosen to show this generation and those to come the way of holiness.

Holiness is an inward experience, and by God's grace and mercy we receive it even though we don't deserve it. Your life has to be dedicated to Christ. When we received His Spirit it empowered us to live free from sin, by the power of God in us. And God assists us in our efforts to overcome sin. God says in His Word, "Ye are of God, little children, and have overcome them: because greater is he that is in you, than he that is in the world" (1 John 4:4). Remember we belong to God; we were redeemed by His blood.

There is a false conception about what holiness is. It is not the way you dress! It is an inside-outward process. If you clean up the outside but the inside has not received God's Spirit, you are still not holy. You have a form of godliness but are denying the power that is within (2 Timothy 3:5). Think about this for a moment; if you put clean clothes on over a dirty body you are still not clean, you only look clean, but you are still dirty on the inside. That is how God feels about putting His new creation into an old vessel with your same dirty ideas. That is why you need to get God's Spirit on the inside so He can wash you and make you white as snow, and make you clean and sanctified.

No one can live holy without God's Spirit which cleanses you of all unrighteousness. We are clean through His Word. He sanctifies His people with the truth. His Word is the truth. God said in John 17:9, "I pray for them: I pray not for the world, but for them which thou hast given me; for they are mine." We are in this world but not of this world. Therefore we should not participate in the things the world does. The Bible calls for a separation from sin. No, it does not mean that you cannot speak to anyone or talk to them. It means you will not do the things they do which are not right according to God's commandments. We do not willfully sin after coming into the knowledge of Jesus.

It is a learning process, because when you are holy you don't see things as the world sees them; we see things in the spirit and they see things in the natural. What the world calls bad or terrible we see as God just trying to get our attention. You have to read God's Word daily. Just as you need regular food to survive, you need God's Word for inner strength. God said, "Man does not live by bread alone, but by every word that proceeds out of the mouth of God" (Matthew 4:4).

The world has become so corrupt and immoral that anything is acceptable. There are random killings and sexual assaults on our children. The moral condition is at its lowest stage right now. Everyone is doing his own thing. It's like what the Bible says about the time when there was no king in Israel and everyone did what was right in his own sight. God's people today must have forgotten we have a King who is keeping this world; the whole world and everything in it is in His hands. Did you know God can get your attention whenever things are out of control? God can shake the whole earth at anytime.

I remember a situation that arose this year that literally shook us. For the first time in our lives we experienced an earthquake in our area. We never have them in Washington, D.C. Everyone was scared. The first thing I heard after it was over was, "I'm glad that is over, now we can get back to normal." The world does not see things the way Christians see them.

The first thought that came to my mind was, *God was just trying to get our attention and let us know He can do whatever He wants, whenever He wants, and anytime He wants.* It's how you perceive things. The Bible says in 1 Corinthians 2-14, "The natural man is not able to receive the things of the Spirit of God for they are foolishness unto him; neither can he know them because they are spiritually discerned."

This is why you who have received God's Spirit and been born again have to allow Him to change your life by following His examples. You have to decrease so He can increase in you. Be willing to submit to Him in order for the change to take place inwardly, and take on His characteristics so God's Spirit can operate in your life. It's the way you look at life that determines your attitude towards life. Holiness is a learning process, and you must be taught to live holy. You have to listen and walk as Jesus did before those who have not come into the knowledge of who Jesus is. Remember it is not an overnight journey.

Your attitude has to change about a lot of things. God is a Spirit and His Spirit lives in you, and when you become that new creature as 2 Corinthians 5:17 says, "where old things are passed away and all things become new," you have to deny some things.

We are told in 2 Timothy 1:13-14, "Hold fast the form of sound words, which thou hast heard of me, in faith and love which is in Christ Jesus. That good thing which was committed unto thee keep by the Holy Ghost which dwelleth in us."

I will always remember what I was taught in Hebrews 2:1 "Therefore we ought to give the more earnest heed to the things which we have heard, lest at any time we should let them slip." It also tells us, "How shall we escape if we neglect so great salvation; which at the first began to be spoken by the Lord, and was confirmed unto us by them that heard him" (v.3). The Word of God is righteous, and you have to take a stand and fight to be righteous. It was written in the days of John the Baptist, "The kingdom of heaven suffered violence and the violent take it by force" (Matthew 11:12). Stop and say this to yourself right now: "I have to put some effort into this!"

You have to grow in God. Remember how faith is developed, by hearing the Word of God. Find a good church and get connected with other believers so your faith can grow.

After you get connected to a good Bible-believing church, this still is an individual walk with God. The Word says, "But they have not all obeyed the gospel, for Esaias saith, Lord, who hath believed our report?" (Romans 14:16). The growing process determines your maturity in God. He expects us to continue to grow in His Word to obtain the strength we need to survive and overcome our problems. Look only to God for His instructions on how to continue your journey. God understands that you are babes in Christ and it is a process. In 1 Peter 2:2-3 it speaks about "the new born babes desiring the sincere milk of the word that you may grow thereby" and how you have to come to Christ like a little child willing to be led (Luke 18:17).

Allow the change to take place in your life that is described in 1 Corinthians 13:11, which says, "When I was a child, I spake as a child, I understood as a child, I thought as a child: but when I became a man, I put away childish things." Conviction must come before conversion. If you want to live this life allow God to empty you of self so He can fill you with His Spirit, and be real in Him.

God knows everything and He knows if you want to learn about Him. The Scripture says He thanked God for you. Matthew 11:25 says, "At that time Jesus answered and said I thank thee, O Father, Lord of heaven and earth, because thou hast hid these things from the wise and prudent, and hast revealed them unto babes."

Stop and think about this for a minute. If one of God's living creatures which He made from the beginning can chew green grass and produce white milk, then why should any other "impossible" thing surprise us? With God all things are possible. Only God can take the impossible and make it possible. So why do you think He cannot take the filth out of you and put in cleanliness?

Before you became born again you did not have God's Spirit to guide you. In 1 Corinthians 6:11 it says, "And such were some of you: but ye are washed, but ye are sanctified, but ye are justified in the name of the Lord Jesus, and by the Spirit of our God." The **blood of Jesus** cleanses us from all sin. God has not called us unto uncleanness, but unto holiness (1 Thessalonians 4:7). Ephesians 1:13 says, "Because we trusted him, after that we heard the Word of Truth, the gospel of salvation, and also believed we were **sealed** with that Holy Spirit of promise." Once you are sealed you are sealed until the day of redemption, and by having this seal the Lord knows them that are His (2 Timothy 2:19).

Now you know you have these promises for the Bible says in 2 Corinthians 7:1, "Having therefore these promises, dearly beloved, let us cleanse ourselves from all filthiness of the flesh and spirit, perfecting holiness in the fear of God. It is written, 'No flesh shall glory in his sight.'"

And Romans 8:13 says, "If ye live after the flesh, ye shall die: but if ye through the Spirit do mortify the deeds of the body, ye shall live." Flesh cannot please God (Romans 8:8). You have to learn how to live holy, but God has already left the instructions. Matthew 11:29-30 says, "Take my yoke upon you, and learn of me; for I am meek and lowly in heart: and ye shall find rest unto your souls. For my yoke is easy, and my burden is light." And there is also a warning from God in Proverbs 16:25 which says, "There is a way that seemeth right unto a man, but the end thereof are the ways of death." You have to know the Word of God for yourself to make the right choices.

Your guide has already been written; you just have to follow it. And remember what He said: "the Comforter, which is the Holy Ghost, whom the Father will send in my name, He shall teach you all things, and bring all things to your remembrance, whatsoever I have said unto you."

Your job is to stand and remember what you have been taught, whether by word or by epistle, and rejoice in the LORD, ye righteous; and give thanks at the "remembrance of his holiness" (Psalm 30:4). Thank God that you were once the servant of sin but now have obeyed the word which was delivered and have been washed in the blood of the Lamb which has delivered you. And finally, let the very God of peace sanctify you wholly (1 Thessalonians 5:23), which means entirely.

Getting Rid of Your Junk

"Stand fast therefore in the liberty wherewith Christ hath made us free, and be not entangled again with the yoke of bondage."
Galatians 5:1

I know all of us can relate to this one, regardless of your status in life, because we **all** have some junk. We had it when we came to God and probably have some right now. Junk is not the things you don't want or which are no longer useful to you. That may be the way the world sees it. But with God it's anything that keeps you from letting His will be done in your life. Yes, it can be an old boyfriend, a so-called church friend, a debt, a car, the way you spend money, not wanting to give your tithes, and that's not all. Junk is anything you put before God.

Some people call the junk a storm. You have heard them say, "I'm going through a storm right now." Depending on what kind of storm it is, it can cause mild to serious damage.

Listen to what God has to say about that junk. Galatians 5:1 says, ". . .stand fast therefore in the liberty wherewith Christ hath made us free, and be not entangled again with the yoke of bondage." It's called bondage, which means you are not free; and you have to know how to get rid of it. God said "He will not suffer you to be tempted above that ye are able; but will with the temptation also make a way to escape, that ye may be able to bear it" (1 Corinthians 10:13).

When you are stuck in a rut and cannot see your way out, that's when you need to stop and take a self-check to see if you are still going in the new direction you had started with Jesus. If not you have to turn around and take that new direction back to Him to find that solid place to stand. God is that place; He is your solid rock, the sure foundation, unmovable, unstoppable, and unrelenting with everlasting strength. Seek Him and stand firm in that situation you are facing which has hindered your walk with God. Be bold and speak to that condition, and trust God to bring you out.

Remember what Jesus said in Mark 11:23-26: have faith in God and speak to your mountains and have no doubt in your hearts, and whatsoever you say those things shall come to pass. You have to face whatever it is. I remember a situation that confronted me, and I knew I had to take a stand otherwise nothing would have changed. Yes, I felt in despair, but then I remembered what God said in 2 Corinthians 4:8-9: "We are troubled on every side, yet not distressed; we are perplexed, but not in despair, persecuted, but not forsaken; cast down, but not destroyed." And God gave me the strength to go through it. The key is to always remember what God has said in His Word about the situation and apply that word over the condition. He is our deliverer.

God has given you the power to cast down imaginations and every high thing that exalts itself against the knowledge of God, and bring every thought into captivity through the obedience of Christ. Remember God said in His Word, "He gives power to the faint and to them who have no might he increases strength" (Isaiah 40:29). Ask Him for it! Jesus gave His life for us and redeemed us from all iniquity, creating us a peculiar people, zealous of good works that we may "speak, and exhort, and rebuke with all authority." And God said, "Let no man despise thee" (Titus 2:14-15). Stand up and use the Word of God!

So when your storms or the junk in your life tries to overpower you, regardless of what it is, take a stand. Think about the kinds of storms we have sometimes—some are mild, some are medium, and some are heavy; they are called hurricanes, tornados, and tsunamis. Some do a little damage and some of them totally destroy everything. It depends on the stand you take when they show up unexpectedly. I know we all have experienced them and are probably going through some right now. But remember no storm lasts forever, does it?

However, during a storm you need to find a place to **stand to be secure** until it passes. Have you noticed when someone comes outside to survey after a storm they look for a secure place to stand so they will not fall down before they begin? That is what God left for us. A sure foundation not made by hands but eternal in the heavens. Because of that foundation you can survive. Yes, it hurts and yes there will be pain, but you are still standing.

You have to go through your storms and hold onto God's hand, trust in Him, and remember what Jesus said in His Word, that "heaven and earth will pass away, but His Word will stand forever." You brought nothing into this world and you will take nothing out. But it is written, "A good man leaveth an inheritance to his children's children: and the wealth of the sinner is laid up for the just" (Proverbs 13:22). That's what God did for us. He gave us Jesus, His only Son, that we may have eternal life. What a gift! He laid down His life that we might live.

Take a stand and ask yourself, is what I'm holding onto worth me giving up Jesus? Remember every house is built by someone, but your house has to be built on a solid foundation, which is the Word of God—no other will stand!

Psalm 127:1 declares, "Except the LORD build the house, they labor in vain that build it: except the LORD keep the city, the watchman waketh but in vain."

We have a spiritual house to build, and it can only stand on a firm foundation built by faith in the Word of God. So be prayerful on how you build. Take an inventory of your junk and get rid of it.

Remember, "If we confess our sins, he is faithful and just to forgive us our sins, and to cleanse us from all unrighteousness" (1 John 1:9).

Walking in the Shadow of God

"He that dwelleth in the secret place of the most High shall abide under the shadow of the Almighty."
(Psalm 91:1)

You should get excited just thinking about such a thing. Can you imagine being in the presence of God all day! It's possible.

The Scripture says, "He that dwelleth in the secret place of the most High shall abide under the shadow of the Almighty" (Psalm 91:1). We are already in that secret place because we have made the Lord, the Most High, our dwelling place. We should not have to fear what shall befall us. He said we can call upon Him at anytime and He will hear, deliver, and honor us! He will deliver us because we love Him and have put our trust in Him, and He knows our name. He has given His angels the charge over us to keep us in all our ways, which means they are responsible for us. The world has their protection and we have ours.

God already knows we will get in trouble because He has been touched with infirmities just like we have and tempted and tested in all points, yet without sin. But because of His Word God said when we fall into temptation to "come boldly to his throne of grace so we can obtain mercy, and find grace to help in our time of trouble" (Hebrews 4:16). There you will find rest for your soul.

I know it's possible to be in God's presence all day. Think about it this way. Go outside and try to run from your shadow. You cannot do it, can you? Your shadow is a part of you. Whenever you move it moves with you. If you fall down it falls down. Wherever you go it will go. Which means God is always with you wherever you go, because we are under the shadow of the Almighty. When I first received God's Spirit the only thing I knew was "He is my Shepherd" and I believed what He said in Psalm 23.

God said He is my Shepherd and that He would provide for me, restore my soul, lead me into the path of righteousness for His name's sake, walk with me when I go through the valley of the shadow of death, and that I would fear no evil for He is with me to comfort me. He said He would set me in the presence of my enemies and anoint my head with oil, and my cup would run over. He assured me that goodness and mercy shall follow me all the days of my life, and I will dwell in His house, the house of the Lord, forever. How could you refuse an invitation like that?

You have been invited to walk with the Almighty God. Which means you will always be in the light. It is important to stay in the light because there is no shadow in darkness. Only light can shine in darkness.

The only time darkness comes into a Christian's life is when he or she has sinned, and the shadow will disappear—because darkness is sin and God hates sin. The Bible says, "God is light and in him is no darkness at all, and if we say we have fellowship and walk in darkness we lie and do not tell the truth, but if we stay in the light we have fellowship, because he cleanses us from all sin" (1 John 1: 4-7).

Darkness makes you feel bad. Have you ever noticed it's like a rainy day? When it rains no one seems to smile, but when the sun comes out everyone rejoices. What a God we have. You need to praise Him for being with you at all times. But if you don't know Him you cannot praise Him.

Stop and think about a time you were in a dark place and how you felt when you came out, or when you saw a little light from God. Did you notice how much difference a little light makes?

I don't know about you but I never start the day without talking to God. And all day I remember He is there, because I can see Him when I walk past a window or anywhere I can see an image. Just imagine that for a minute. It brings chills down your spine, doesn't it? You are never alone because God is there all the time.

It feels so good to know He is always right there protecting, guiding, instructing, and covering you; if you look to Him for guidance He is that close to you.

Sometimes we need to do a self-check to see where we have taken our shadow lately. Ask yourself, would God be pleased? Remember He was there and also heard and saw what you did or said.

Many of us have become so concerned about what people think of us, or what they would say, that we have forgotten about the person we are really supposed to please—the Almighty God, our Creator, the one who gave His life for us so we could live. Do you remember Him? The all-knowing everlasting God?

We can love and respect our peers without going to some of the places they go and doing some of the things they do. God said in His Word, "Marvel not, my brethren, if the world hates you, because we know we have passed from death unto life, because we still love them, even if they do things we don't do" (1 John 3:13-14). God did not say to isolate yourself. He gave us a mind to guide us. Remember, "Let this mind be in you which is also in Christ Jesus." Don't take God anywhere you feel it would condemn your walk with Him. "Abstain from all appearance of evil" (1 Thessalonians 5:22).

The Word says, "If in this life only we have hope in Christ we are of all men most miserable," which simply means we are to seek those things above, because where your treasure is there your heart will be also. I Timothy 6:6 says, "But godliness with contentment is great gain." Learn to wait on God. He said He would bless you "exceedingly abundantly above all we could ask or think according to the power that worketh in us" (Ephesians 3:20).

God warned us to "love not the world, neither the things that are in the world, for the love of the Father is not in them. Because the lust of the flesh, and the lust of the eyes, and the pride of life is not of the Father, but is of the world, and the world will pass away and lust there of: but whoever doeth the **will** of God abideth for ever" (1 John 2:15-17). What you seek will become your God. The Bible says to seek ye first the kingdom of God and all these things will be added unto you. Remember God already knows what your needs are; you cannot fool Him.

Even your tithes already belong to God, and He sees what you do. It was not easy for me in the beginning because I saw the natural before the spiritual—the bills rather than something I could not see—but I am learning to be obedient to God first and take whatever comes after. Because there will come a time when the money gets funny, but you will survive because He is a God of provision. And all things work together for good to those who are called according to His purpose.

That is why that shadow stays over you, to remind you "I am here." When you suffer God suffers, so you are not going through it alone. Remember, where you go He goes, so be careful where you take Him. He is a jealous God! Give honor to whom honor is due. Honor God!

Making an Impact

> *"And of some have compassion,*
> *making a difference."*
> *(Jude 1:22)*

The Bible says we are living epistles read of all men. Which means after you say you have been born again people watch your walk to see if it lines up with your talk! If you don't believe this make a mistake.

My husband and I were taking a Bible class and met a man named John Ola who said he walked by faith. I never heard John say God was not able to handle anything in his life, even when he was going through difficult situations. He always gave God the glory. His walk matched his talk. My husband and I would pray with John after class and believe God for answers to both our situations and his. He made an impact on our lives because of the stand he took to believe God through whatever. God honors faith!

A Christian's life is a looking-glass. Others will always be watching you. No, you are not perfect, but you belong to God and they are looking to see a difference. If you profess you are saved your life should be an example so others can see there has been a change in your life.

We are living in a time when churches are changing the Word of God to make people feel good. You don't hear much about being sanctified or about hell and fearing God anymore. They want to take out that part. But the Bible tells me that God hates sin and injustice.

That is why He sent His Son into the world to redeem us from it by the washing of His blood to cleanse all our sin, so we would not fall into damnation. And, yes, we are living under grace now, but do not tempt God!

When religion does not have Jesus' true Word in it, it's empty and lacks purpose. When we go to church we go to hear the truth so we can apply it to our lives that others might see the difference in our walk and find their way too.

We are to speak boldly about our salvation and who made us free. God is our Savior; He died on the cross and shed His blood that we might live free from sin in this sinful world. For our conversation is in heaven, whence also we look for the Savior, our Lord Jesus Christ for everything (Philippians 3:20). It is written, "For it is not ye that speak but the Spirit of your Father which speaketh in you" (Matthew 10:20). Those whom God has sent speak of Him.

The things of this world don't have power over us anymore because we are the righteousness of God and not of the law for we are living by grace through faith and the mercy of God (Philippians 3:7-9).

Our conversations should be enlightening so others can see the difference Christ has made in our life and want to be partakers also. When things go wrong in our life, we need to rejoice over the situation because of our belief in Jesus to bring us out. You don't have to look down and out if you truly believe what the Word says: that our God will supply all our needs according to His riches in glory in Christ Jesus.

Yes, Jesus is a mystery. That is why we approach things differently than the world. We can go through our afflictions and sufferings because of His Spirit and stay grounded and settled in Him (Colossians 2:2-3). We are confident that no philosophy or vain traditions of men or the cares of this world can change our walk with Christ because of the hope in us—we are complete in Him. We lack nothing. Remember all good and perfect gifts come from above.

We were buried with Him in baptism and risen with Him through faith, and all our sins have been blotted out. Therefore we have a story to tell to the unsaved that He lives because He lives in us, and our walk must match up with what we say. We are imbued with the very Spirit of God!

We are to walk worthy, put off the old things, mortify them, and set our affections on things above, not what we see on this earth, because there is only "one God and Father of all, who is above all, and through all, and in all" (Colossians 3:2). We have to put on the bowels of mercy and control what we do and say before the world because they are always watching. Ask God to open your understanding and help you walk in wisdom towards those without, and let your "speech be with grace and seasoned with salt that we may know how to answer any man that asks us about this salvation plan" (Colossians 4:6). We must remember that we are the salt of the earth, but if the salt has lost it flavor it is good for nothing. Salt is for seasoning to make things taste better. Our God is good and full of flavor. The Bible says, "O taste and see that the Lord is good, blessed is the man that trusteth in Him" (Psalm 34:8).

Your life is to show others by the **stand you have taken** that there is another way than to continue on the way which leads to destruction. James 5:20 says that whosoever turns a sinner from the error of his way shall save a soul from death, and shall hide a multitude of sins.

The Word has already been written; nothing can be added to it and nothing taken away. We cannot be ashamed to tell the story of Jesus Christ, because the Word says, "We are not ashamed of the gospel of Christ: for it is the power of God unto salvation to every one that believeth" (Romans 1:16). It is written, "Whosoever believeth on him shall not be ashamed" (Romans 10:11).

We are ambassadors for Christ, and we are on a mission to tell the world about Jesus Christ and that He lives, because He is living in us. So that old phrase about "you get what you see" and "what goes up must come down" is right. You will get Jesus! Why? Because He went up to prepare a place for us so that where He is we may be also, and He is coming again to receive all those who have been redeemed and have received Him.

Jesus said, "If I be lifted up from the earth, I will draw all men unto me" (John 12:32). Our job is to lift up the name of Jesus so others might see, and He will do the drawing.

Chapter Four

Recognizing the Devil and Overcoming His Tactics

How the Devil Operates

"Lest Satan should get an advantage of us: for we are not ignorant of his devices."
(2 Corinthians 2:11)

First we must recognize what we need to see to defeat the devil. We know his name, but we also need to know how he operates. The Word of God tells us that Satan is deceitful, cunning, and most of all a transformer and impersonator, which means he is like a chameleon, a lizard that can change colors corresponding to its environment. He can turn himself into anything he wants to be— in other words just what you are looking for to get you hooked. You will not be able to recognize him if you don't know his tactics. Yes, he is a spirit and needs a body to function in, and he will use whoever surrenders their body to him. That is why the Bible says to "try the spirits to see if they are of God" (1 John 4:1). Ask God for His Holy Spirit to lead and guide you, because you need to be equipped to defeat the devil.

When Jesus' ministry on earth drew to a close, He prayed to the Father for His disciples one final time to bestow blessings upon them that they would be kept from evil. And this applies to us today too, because we are Jesus' disciples, His church which God has given Him on earth to keep from evil (John 17:15-24).

That prayer is still significant for us today because we live in a world that is filled with evil designs of the adversary the devil, who is our enemy. And we must maintain a higher standard of life as a true believer in Christ. As a believer you carry God's Holy Spirit, and you have to be aware of your attitude and how you respond or deal with situations in your life. Remember what the Lord told Peter in Luke 22:31: "Simon, Simon, behold, Satan hath desired to have you, that he may sift you as wheat: But I have prayed for thee, that thy faith fail not: and when thou art converted, strengthen thy brethren."

So I am writing this to inform you, brothers and sisters, about what I heard. There is a war going on, and never before has there been greater evidence of that war between the powers of heaven and the forces of evil than right now. We as God's chosen people need to recognize that this war is not for territory or wealth, but a contest for the eternal souls of men, women, and children who are the offspring of God.

We must realize how serious this conflict is. Have you really looked at your family lately? Do you understand what the devil is trying to do to us? Our children are being demonized by the things they see on television, or what I call "hell in vision," and other media outlets are doing the same thing. Our children have become ungodly and unruly because they are being influenced by what they see secular role models do and say: how they dress, how they speak, and how they act in general. Most of them are worldly examples and not spiritual, and surely not of God.

The devil knows a church that can keep out the spirit of worldliness is a spiritually strong church. Yes, the devil goes to church just like you. Do you remember when God held a prayer meeting and the devil came? The book of Job (1:6) reminds us about the devil. It says, "Now there was a day when the sons of God came to present themselves before the LORD, and Satan came also among them." Jude 1:4 says, "For there were certain men who crept in unawares, ungodly men, turning the grace of our God into lasciviousness, and denying the only Lord God, and our Lord Jesus Christ." God said that about the Laodicean church, which had allowed worldliness to creep into it. God said, "I know thy works, that thou art neither cold nor hot: I would thou wert cold or hot. So then because thou art lukewarm, and neither cold nor hot, I will spue thee out of my mouth" (Revelation 3:15-16). You cannot fool God. We have been warned to love not the world, neither the things that are in it (1 John 2:15).

Do you recognize the devil's emissaries for what they are when they openly assail to seduce and destroy you quietly? Do you? Take a stand and dare to be different! Proverbs 12:21 tells us, "There shall no evil happen to the just: but the wicked shall be filled with mischief." The Word also says in 2 Timothy 3:13, "Evil men and seducers shall wax worse and worse, deceiving, and being deceived." Always be alert!

Have you stopped to realize how much the devil has used that weapon of seduction in his efforts to destroy God's people? It's alluring and appears to be advantageous at the same time it is destroying your soul. Spiritual seduction will make you think bitter is sweet and black is white and that sin is acceptable and virtue is obsolete (Isaiah 5:20-23). Isaiah said, "Woe unto them who do this." Which means great sorrow will come upon them. For it justifies sin for a reward and takes away the righteousness in you. You must remember that the devil revels in filth. He will whisper that to be clean is some old concept of your grandmother's era, and it does not apply in this enlightened age. He is a liar! The Bible says so. He is "the father of lies" and knows not the truth. "There is no truth in him because he was a liar from the beginning" (John 8:44).

We must spend time earnestly seeking to overcome evil and to become as much like Christ as possible. You cannot do this halfheartedly for Satan is skillful in his efforts to drag our souls down to hell. But God's power is greater, and with His help and our sincere efforts we can live pure in a world dominated by sin. God said you are of God and have overcome them; because "greater is he that is in you than he that is in the world" (1 John 4:4). Yes, this world belongs to Satan, because he is the prince of the air, but God has control over it because He also made Satan.

The lies Satan tells are the same ones he has used before. He will tell you standards have changed and are more relaxed. Go ahead and do your own thing, express your desires, have fun, let yourself go, let your hair down—and if you believe him you are hooked.

Do you recognize him when he comes with a soft voice and a disarming smile? Do you recognize evil when you see it? Do you really know right from wrong?

The devil deceived Eve in the Garden of Eden when he told her that she could eat from all the trees in the garden, even the one God had warned her not to eat from, and she believed him by the way the devil presented it to her. She ate from the tree and also persuaded Adam to eat. God had given Adam all authority to keep the garden, but he yielded to Satan's words and disobeyed God's warning. Why? The devil is a deceiver; he twisted the words when he was speaking to Eve, and Eve told Adam the way the devil presented it to her. Adam did not recognize the devil because he believed Eve (Genesis 3:2-4). You have to watch how anything is presented to you if it involves changing the Word of God in any way.

The teachings we hear today have conformed more and more to be acceptable to what people want to hear rather than what the actual Word of God said from the beginning. Even church members may be confused about some issues that confront them. A lot of social issues threaten moral decay and have a powerful effect upon our families—including abortion, flexible marriage laws, and permissiveness in what we read and view in the media. We are told this is good for society, which is not true. God's Word has already been written on those subjects, and it has never changed regardless of how the world presents it.

God said in Malachi 3:6, "I am the LORD, I change not; therefore ye sons of Jacob are not consumed." This means we will still be standing and not destroyed. Matthew 24:35 proclaims that heaven and earth would pass away, but His Word will **stand forever**. And Romans 1:25 speaks of those "who changed the truth of God into a lie, and worshipped and served the creature more than the Creator, who is blessed for ever."

Once sin enters your life it takes control and you are no more you, but whatever it wants you to be. You have to remember to whomever you yield yourself, you become that person's servant, whether of sin unto death, or obedience unto righteousness. Romans

8:6 is your reminder: "for to be carnally minded is death; but to be spiritually minded is life and peace." A carnal man or woman walks after the flesh, but a spiritual man or woman walks after the Spirit.

David knew when he had sinned against God, and so do we. David asked God to create in him a clean heart and renew in him a right spirit, because he knew he was out of God's will for his life and that sin had taken over. You have to do the same. Sin is contrary to the spirit.

The church has some great actors. We come to church and put on a smile, but when we leave we are still bound. We need to stop, take a stand, and acknowledge there is a problem so we can be delivered. The wrong people in your life can take you to places you don't want to go. There are some who know just how to do everything, but they are **not real** with themselves. Yes, there is a "real you" in all of us! But will the **real you stand up and take authority?** God is trying to get us to the point where we can recognize and confess our weaknesses. He knows there is a war going on, and only God can deliver you. Take authority over that devil and expose him.

God knew we would be confronted for standing for the name of Jesus. He said, "Think it not strange concerning the fiery trial which is to try you" (1 Peter 4:12). He said to be aware because the devil your adversary is walking about seeking whom he may devour: but you are to resist him, be steadfast in your faith, because after you have suffered awhile God will make you perfect, establish, strengthen, and settle you, because of the true grace of God wherein you stand. God said "he that committed sin is of the devil; for the devil sinneth from the beginning." And for this purpose the Son of God was manifested, that he might destroy the works of the devil (1 John 3:8).

Jesus told us what the thief came to do in John 10:10: "The thief cometh not, but for to steal, and to kill, and to destroy: I am come that they might have life, and that they might have it more abundantly." We know the devil's tactics because we have been warned in 2 Corinthians 2:11, which says, "Lest Satan should get an advantage of us: for we are not ignorant of his devices." And God did not leave us defenseless; He left all His believers the armor of God

(Ephesians 6:10-18). Jesus knew we would need some powerful weapons to stand.

The armor of God consists of certain components, and Jesus (writing through the apostle Paul) instructed us on how to use them.

> Finally, my brethren, be strong in the Lord, and in the power of his might. Put on the whole armor of God that ye may be able to withstand in the evil day against the wiles of the devil, for we wrestle not against flesh and blood, but stand against principalities, against powers, against rulers of the darkness of this world, against spiritual wickedness in high places. Wherefore take unto you the whole armor of God, and having done all, to stand. Stand therefore, having your loins girt about with truth, and having on the breastplate of righteousness, and your feet shod with the preparation of the gospel of peace. Above all, taking the shield of faith with you, so you will be able to quench all the fiery darts of the wicked. And take the helmet of salvation, and the sword of the Spirit, which is the **word of God**.

Remember you have to defend yourself. Use those weapons; we are in a war! We cannot defeat the enemy by throwing marshmallows; the devil is throwing bricks. He does not want to just wound you, he wants to kill you. You need the ROCK, Jesus Christ, and use His name the way David used it!

Take a stand, because we are ambassadors for Jesus and are defending the kingdom of God, which no man can pull down. God made this world, and He is the King over everything in it including the ruler of darkness, the devil.

The Word of God says that when the devil comes in like a flood, many will not recognize him. Why? Because he was not red and wearing horns like you thought. He changed your attitude, your conversation, and confused your life; envy and strife entered, your peace disappeared, and your children and family came under attack because you changed your direction from God. How? You let the devil get into your mind. Did you forget what God said, "Thou wilt keep him in **perfect** peace, whose mind is stayed on thee: because he trusteth in thee" (Isaiah 26:3).

Now it's time to take a stand and put that devil out. God wants His people to be reminded to put on the armor and go to battle for your life and family. God is not the author of confusion; read it again (1 Corinthians 14:33): "For God is not the author of **confusion**, but of peace, as in all churches of the saints." God wants His people to know this has already been written for their guidance, and He repeated it again in James 3:16: "For where envying and strife is, there is **confusion** and every evil work." You have to remember the instructions God left for you to defeat this devil.

God ordained the family, and He instructed you in His Word on how to manage what He left in your authority. In the beginning when God created the heaven and earth He spoke all things into existence except Adam and Eve. And when He told them to go forth and multiply He was not just referring to having a family. Everything man could think of was available to him.

Today the devil has launched such an attack on God's family they have lost their jobs and their homes, and their children have become disobedient, and if you don't use what's in your hand like God told Moses in the wilderness, you will not be able to stand. You have to use the gift God gave you to create your own job to support your family.

Some of us, if not all, right now are at a crossroads in our lives and need to find a place to stand and work out this situation. We have forgotten we have the mind of Christ and can create anything with the help of Almighty God. Man is very smart in his own way, but he has forgotten who gave him that mind to create all the things we use every day to survive. Think about it; they were created by someone. And every day someone is coming up with another new thing or another new invention. God gave me the vision to write this book! Praise His name!

The knowledge to build anything does not come from man or woman. If God had not given them the thought and the mind to create, how would they be able to do it? The time has come for you to use the gift God gave you to support your family. Don't let pride or what anyone else says hinder you when your family's survival is threatened.

Take that stand and take back your family from the devil. God will be with whatever you do if you trust Him. The Word says in 3 John 1:2, "Beloved, I wish above all things that thou mayest prosper and be in health, even as thy soul prospereth."

Remember you *can* recover from an attack by the devil. You may come out with some bruises but you will still be standing, because "all things work together for good for those who love the Lord and are called according to his purpose" (Romans 8:28).

Now, you know you are called, but do you know your purpose? After you have learned how to live holy by the grace of God, and recognize that there is a dark force of evil out there to prevent God's people from getting their inheritance (entering the kingdom of God to receive eternal life), you are to warn your brothers and sisters that we can defeat the devil by [pleading the blood over your family] submitting to God and resisting the devil. "He will flee from you" (James 4:7). Recognize who you are in Jesus. We are those who have been washed in the blood of the Lamb and are not afraid of losing anything to hold onto God, because we have learned to **stand, take authority, and never doubt.**

You have been chosen for this season, and you have to take that stand. Either choose sin for a season or God for eternity.

False Doctrines

> *"Beloved, believe not every spirit, but try the spirits whether they are of God: because many false prophets are gone out into the world."*
> *(1 John 4:1)*

We are living in the last days, and the Bible is being fulfilled every day. God's Word says that "in the last days there shall be false prophets and teachers arising and deceiving many, and they shall shew great signs and wonders, and if possible they shall fool the very elect" (Matthew 24:24). But we who know God and have been taught the truth must remember what God said about this situation.

You are to try the spirits to see if they are of God. He told us to take heed and let no man deceive us.

Yes, many deceivers are already out in the world deceiving God's people. But we know that "every spirit that confesseth that Jesus Christ is come in the flesh is of God: and every spirit that confesseth not that Jesus Christ is come in the flesh is not of God: which is the spirit of antichrist" (1 John 4:2-3). If you get connected to the wrong spirits, which are not of God, iniquity will enter your life and your love will wax cold because you will no longer be walking in the love of God. You have to endure to the end to be saved.

God said not to be "beguiled by enticing words, and let no man spoil you with philosophy and vain deceit, and the traditions of men and not of God by the rudiments of the world and not after Christ, to please their own fleshly knowledge. For these are those who separate themselves, sensual, having not the Spirit" (Jude 1:19). "And they speak evil of things which they know not: but what they know naturally and corrupt themselves," and much sorrow will happen to them because of their greed, and they will perish because they have left the core (Jude 1:10-11). And if you believe them you will be drawn away from the true God, the one who shed His blood that you might inherit eternal life.

We have to know the speech patterns of those who profess they know God. If they don't speak love and deny God, they don't know Him. They speak what they know which is of the world. That is why we must be sure we are hearing the voice of God from a true shepherd and His servants, for only the Lord's servants can inform and guide us away from false doctrines. Compare what you are hearing to the Word of God. That's what the Bible is for. It's your roadmap with all the instructions God left for you to follow to receive eternal life.

Eternal truth never changes. It is written that heaven and earth will pass away but God's Word will stand forever! He said, "My sheep know my voice, and I know them, and they follow me" (John 10:27). We will not hear or follow a spirit that is not of God. We are connected after being born again and receiving His Spirit, and we listen and are guided by that Spirit.

Jude 1:17 says, "Remember ye the words which were spoken before of the apostles of our Lord Jesus Christ." Those whom God has sent will speak the words of God, for it is God who speaks through him (John 3:34).

The Bible says in 1 Peter 4:11, "If any man speak, let him speak as the oracles of God; and minister under the ability as God giveth, that God in all things may be glorified through Jesus Christ, to whom be praise and dominion for ever and ever." The end of all things is at hand, and we are told to be sober, and watch unto prayer (1 Peter 4:7).

Anything that leads you away from God is not of God. You have to humble yourself, pray, and ask God to guide you in the right direction and keep you away from evil forces. Remain in His will and let nothing pull you away. We are seeking eternal life, which only comes from Jesus Christ and living for Him. He is our hope of glory.

You have to study God's Word so you will not be deceived. We have been warned about false prophets and teachers in the last days, and some of God's people will depart from the faith, giving into false doctrine and seducing spirits, doctrines of devils. But we were warned not to be carried away by them (Hebrews 13:9).

In 2 Peter 2:2 it says, "But there were false prophets also among the people, even as there shall be false teachers among you, who privily shall bring in damnable heresies, even denying the Lord that bought them, and bring upon themselves swift destruction." Knowing God's Word will keep you from being deceived.

A true shepherd of God will teach you how to recognize things that are not according to the Scripture. God did leave some instructions in place for the work of the ministry, to counsel and help with the "perfecting of the saints, and to edify the body of Christ" (Ephesians 4:11-12).

God does not want His people to be tossed to and fro and carried away by false doctrine delivered by false prophets in their cunning craftiness and deceitfulness, but to be united in faith, unity, and the knowledge of truth, speaking the love of Christ, until we all come into the fullness of who Christ really is in our life.

When I first came to Christ I thought everybody who professed Jesus in the church and outside the church was saved and knew Him. Then I saw some things that did not quite line up with what the Bible says. Remember we are epistles read of all men, and where you are getting your Christian information determines how you grow in God's Word.

The book of 1 Peter (4:17) talks about "the time is now that judgment should begin at the house of God: and if it begins with us what shall the end be of them that obey not the gospel of God?" You have to know the true Word of God.

The answer is already given in verse 18: "If the righteous **scarcely** be saved, where shall the ungodly and the sinner appear?"

Try those spirits as the Bible says to see if they are of God. No one is perfect, but we should be asking God every day to take anything which is not of Him away so we will not be false representatives of Christ. The Spirit inside of you guides you into all truth and understanding. Ask God for the gift of discernment so you will be able to see those things which are not of God.

Be aware of where you are getting your teachings, and give no place to the devil!

If It's New Is It True?

> *"And I John saw the holy city, new Jerusalem coming down from God out of heaven prepared as a bride adorned for her husband. And he that sat upon the throne said, Behold I make all things new. And he said unto me, Write for these words are true and faithful."*
> *(Revelation 21:2, 5)*

Is everything you see now being called new in God's name true? It is written that what God is doing has already been here before. If you listen to the Spirit as you read this, you should know that what some people are calling new is not true. Ecclesiastes 3:15-17 says "that which hath been is now; and that which is to be hath already been; and God requires that which is past." There is a time and a season for everything God has said from the beginning and what is happening now to come to pass, because this is the appointed time for history to fulfill itself. The Bible says "you shall know the truth and the truth shall make you free" (John 8:32).

Do you remember how you came into **being** and how you arrived where you are now? You need to know who you are and whose you are.

Genesis is our source on how we were created. It says in the beginning God created the heaven and the earth, and the earth was void and dark. Then God's Spirit moved upon the face of the water, and He began to speak all things into existence, and there was not **anything made** which was not made by **Him.** God set everything in place and looked at it and said it was **good**!

It is written how God created man in His own image from the dust of the earth and breathed in his nostrils, and he became a living soul. He created a garden eastward and placed the man in the garden to dress and keep it and have dominion over everything in it. And He gave him a commandment about what he could freely eat from all the trees in the garden except the tree of knowledge of good and evil, because the day he did he would surely die. Then out of the ground God formed every living creature and fowl of the air and brought them to Adam, and he named each one of them. If you noticed, whenever God created any fowl of the air or living creature He always created male and female so they could reproduce. God's Word has not changed since He spoke it in the beginning regarding **His creation**.

Then God noticed there was no help meet for man because there was no one like him. Leviticus 18:22 says, "Thou shalt not lie with mankind, as with womankind, it is an abomination." So God caused a deep sleep to fall upon Adam and took a rib from his side and made a woman and brought her to Adam, and he called her woman because she was taken out of man. God blessed them and told them to be fruitful and multiply.

He placed them in the Garden of Eden, the place prepared for them to live. God knew the devil was also in the garden. God was testing them to see if they could keep His commandments during temptation.

When the first temptation came it was through Eve. The devil changed the Word of God and beguiled Eve to eat from the forbidden fruit tree in the garden, and she persuaded Adam to eat also. Sisters, you know how we can be! But this broke the commandment between Adam and God. And when the evening came, they heard God's voice calling to them as He walked in the garden, and they became afraid because their conscience had been awakened and their **eyes opened** from eating from the tree of knowledge of good and evil, and they realized they had broken the commandment of God. Now they could see things differently because they had become **aware** of their being, and they were now seeing things in the **flesh,** not by the **spirit** anymore.

The Scripture says God asked Adam "where are you?" Adam and Eve were hiding because they were naked. And then God asked Adam, "Did you eat from the forbidden tree?"

> And the LORD God said unto the serpent, God said, "Because thou hast done this, thou art cursed above all cattle, and above every beast of the field; upon thy belly shalt thou go, and dust shalt thou eat all the days of thy life: And I will put enmity between thee and the woman, and between thy seed and her seed; it shall bruise thy head, and thou shalt bruise his heel: and unto the woman he said, I will greatly multiply thy sorrow and thy conception; in sorrow thou shalt bring forth children; and thy desire shall be to thy husband, and he shall rule over thee: and unto Adam he said, Because thou hast hearkened unto the voice of thy wife, and hast eaten of the tree, of which I commanded thee, saying, Thou shalt not eat of it: cursed is the ground for thy sake; in sorrow shalt thou eat of it all the days of thy life." Genesis 3:14-17.

You should take heed from this story how the devil has always tried to destroy God's work, but he must have forgotten that God said, "I am the great I am and besides me there is no other."

Always remember whatever the devil can do God can repair. Adam and Eve knew they were wrong, and you also have to realize when you are wrong. And at some point in your life stop being fooled by the devil's tactics.

It's imperative that you return to the Old Testament and read the book of Genesis. It's our genealogy. The first ten chapters tells about the creation and the rise and fall of man and how God had to destroy the world He had made and create a new one because of sin. In the New Testament, in Jude 1:5, it reads, "I will therefore put you in remembrance, though ye once knew this, how the Lord, having saved the people out of the land of Egypt, afterward destroyed them that believed not." You have to remember and believe what the Word of God says about whatever is happening now.

Before we came into the knowledge of Christ we used to say "if this does not work, I have plan A or B," and for some of us we probably had many more. That is not the way God's people think, because whatever God makes is shatter-proof, and it is forever, because we know how to start over again. God had to do it.

In Genesis you will find Noah and Abraham, two men of great faith who found God's favor, and He made covenants with them and called them friend because of their walk and keeping His commandments. God trusted them and started to build again after the fall of Adam and the flood.

From that point on God chose people like Moses and Joshua who had found grace in His sight; He filled them with wisdom, understanding, and knowledge to continue on the journey with the people God had sworn unto Abraham, Isaac, and Jacob into the **new land** He had prepared for them (Genesis 33). The Bible tells us "it flowed with milk and honey." But like some of us today they murmured and turned back. I heard you have to stay focused to make this journey.

I know this was in the Old Testament and under the law, and today we are living under grace, but God wants you to know His Word has not changed since He spoke it in the beginning. It is written, "I am God and I change not." And "my word is forever settled in heaven" (Psalm 119:89).

This is what the Word of God says about what is being called new. Jude 1:3 says, "Beloved when I gave all diligence to write unto you of the common salvation, it was needful for me to write unto you, and exhort you that ye should earnestly contend for the faith which was once delivered unto the saints."

Jude knew there would come a time when we would have to make a decision about our faith and trust in God, because the old covenant could not be fulfilled and God had to make a better covenant to complete the old one.

He was warning us that some new things were coming which would change how we receive the Word of God, because of **new teachings** we would receive from **ungodly men** who crept in, changing the gospel for their own good and denying God's Word.

But He said you know the Lord and to remember who saved you. Don't be like the people in the cities of Sodom and Gomorrah who walked away from God and suffered the vengeance of eternal fire, but remember the words which were spoken before of the apostles of our Lord Jesus Christ, and separate yourself from them who walk not according to God's Word.

Matthew 28:20 says, "God is the only one who can keep you from falling, and present you faultless before the presence of his glory with exceeding joy, because he is the only wise God and our Saviour." And He has given you a **"new way of living,** which He hath consecrated for us, through the veil, that is to say His flesh" (Hebrews 10:20).

The Bible tells us **God makes all things new:** He said to "write these words because they are true and faithful" (Revelation 21:1-5). And the new commandment God gave to us was that "we should love one another" (John 13:34).

The new thing God was referring to was the **new creature**, His **redeemed church,** after you became born again. As 2 Corinthians 5:17 says, "Old things will pass away and behold all things become new." And you will become that new man or woman God created in righteousness and **true holiness** (Ephesians 4:24). And every day you will have "new mercies given to you each and every morning" (Lamentations 3:3). Peter tell us "nevertheless we, according to his promise, should look for a **new heaven and a new earth,** wherein dwelleth righteousness" (2 Peter 3:13).

God said "that which was from the beginning, which we have heard, which we have seen with our eyes, which we have looked upon, and our hands have handled, of the Word of life" (1 John 1:1) has not changed; it's still God's Word.

It is written, "Now to him that is of power to stablish you according to my gospel, and the preaching of Jesus Christ, according to the revelation of the mystery, which was kept secret since the world began" (Romans 16:25). God said, "I write no new commandment unto you, but an old commandment which ye had from the beginning. The old commandment is the Word which you have heard from the beginning" (1 John 2:7-8).

"The thing that hath been it is that which shall be; and that which is done is that which shall be done: and there is **no new thing under the sun**" (Ecclesiastes 1:9). The Scripture goes on to say, "Is there anything whereof it may be said, See, this is new? "It hath been already of old time which was before us" (v.10).

So if it's new is it true? It is **God's Word,** and it **has been here before** the foundation of the world. The Old Testament under the law was a shadow of things to come—it concealed. And the New Testament under God's grace tells you what is now—it reveals.

God made the new covenant because the first one under the law had become decayed and waxed old, and He said it "would vanish away so all things can become new." And instead he gave us the New Testament, which is under grace because He shed His blood for the remission of our sins (Matthew 26:28). Now we can live covered by the blood of Jesus. We are connected to Jesus through the bloodline.

You have to know your **history:** how you began and how you will end according to the Word of God. Both the Old and New Testament should be read. We did not start out in the New Testament; we are living the things which the Old Testament said would come to pass. You have to know your bloodline—we are Abraham's seed.

From the beginning God talked with Abraham and told him He was the Almighty and "if thou walk before me and be thou perfect I will make a covenant between me and thee and will multiply thee exceedingly, and thou shall become the father of many nations" (Genesis 17:1-5).

And Genesis 17:19 says, "His seed which would come forth in Isaac he would make a covenant with that seed and it would be an **everlasting covenant** and also with his **seed after him**." We are the seed of Abraham, the father of many nations. We are that one nation under God, and in God we trust.

If you don't know where you started, how will you know how this story began, and how can you have hope for the ending? Did you forget who you are supposed to be following to get to where you are going? Yes, we are living under the new covenant and not by the law anymore, because 2 Corinthians 3:6 says, "Who also hath made us able ministers of the New Testament; not of the letter, but of the Spirit: for the letter **killeth**, but the Spirit giveth life." But you cannot have one without the other, and you need to understand how they are connected. We are connected with Jesus by His DNA. Blood had to touch blood. Do you know whose blood you are living by, and whose DNA? **Did you forget about the bloodline?**

I became so overwhelmed when I wrote this part of the book I began to tremble. I was overshadowed by the Spirit of God and did not know what was happening to me, so I sat down and asked God. Then I heard a voice say, "This is that which was prophesied by the prophet Joel."

> **And it shall come to pass afterward, that I will pour out my spirit upon all flesh; and your sons and your daughters shall prophesy, your old men shall dream dreams, your young men shall see visions: And also upon the servants and upon the handmaids in those days will I pour out my spirit.**
>
> **Joel 2:28-29**

Don't forget to "hold fast the sound words, which you have been taught in faith and love for Jesus." Stay committed to be "kept by the Holy Ghost which dwelleth in you" (1 Timothy 1:9-14). And remember there is nothing new under the sun except what the Father told us. He made a promise to all of us, after we believed and became that new creature in Christ. He promised us "a new heaven, a new earth and eternal life."

Hosea 4:6 says, "**My people** are destroyed for lack of knowledge; because thou hast rejected knowledge, I will also reject thee, that thou shalt be no priest to me: seeing thou hast forgotten the law of thy God, I will also forget thy children."

God's Word has never changed, and His Spirit is still speaking to His people and saying the same thing. "If my people who are called by my name, shall humble themselves, and pray, and seek my face, and turn from their wicked ways; then will I hear from heaven, and will forgive their sin, and will heal their land" (2 Chronicles 7:14). Are you listening?

It is written, "He that hath an **ear**, let him hear what the Spirit saith unto the churches; and to him that overcometh will I give to eat of the hidden manna, and will give him a white stone, and in the stone a new name written, which no man knoweth saving he that receiveth it" (Revelation 2:17).

It's not new, it's been here before; therefore we should not forget the old landmark but rejoice in the **new thing God is doing** with His **newly redeemed people** on whom He has poured out His Spirit in these last days. We realize that with Him we can do all things and nothing is impossible. We are the **REAL** church of **REAL** people, believing in a **REAL God**. We are His new generation of believers, believing on the same Word He left in the beginning. The Scripture tells us God made heaven and earth, and everything He created or spoke into existence was good.

Romans 8:25 tells us, "But if we hope for that we see not, then do we with patience wait for it." Like Abraham after he had patiently endured, he obtained the promise (Hebrews 6:15). And Luke 12:2 says, "For there is nothing covered that shall not be revealed; neither hid, that shall not be known."

We are reminded in 1 Thessalonians 5:21-22 "to prove all things; hold fast that which is good and abstain from all appearance of evil." And also to remember what is written in Romans 15:4, "for whatsoever things were written afore time were written for our learning, that we through patience and comfort of the scriptures might have **hope**." God is your hope!

Chapter Five

Conclusion: Victory

You Have the Victory

"But thanks be to God, which giveth us the victory through our Lord Jesus Christ."
(1 Corinthians 15:57)

When you accepted Jesus into your life and became born again you received the victory. And when you totally surrendered to God He gave you the power to overcome the **REAL** you. Now you have to stand and become that real person, not the one you used to be, or the other one people wanted you to be, but the one God created you to be. Your victory came from knowing the victor, who is Jesus Christ, and you only have to please Him.

When I first received Jesus, I didn't realize how powerful He was. But the more I learned about Him, obeyed, trusted, and applied His Word, and allowed Him to make me into what He wanted me to be, I became stronger and stronger and have been able to stand through many afflictions by His grace and mercy. Is it easy? No. Does it work? Yes! I am still standing. I am a witness.

Remember you have to ask God for help! He shed His blood so we could overcome and have eternal life. Revelation 12:11 reads, "And they overcame him by the blood of the Lamb and by the word of their testimony; and they loved not their lives unto the death."

Which means even faced with death they did not choose their life over death. The devil wants your testimony! Remember to always stand; don't give in to him!

It is written in Hebrews 2:14-15, "Forasmuch then as the children are partakers of flesh and blood, he also himself likewise took part of the same; that through death he might destroy him that had the power of death, that is, the devil; and deliver them who through fear of death were all their life subject to bondage." Jesus is talking about you and me.

The devil is already defeated. Psalm 8:2 says, "Out of the mouth of babes and sucklings hast thou ordained strength because of thine enemies, that thou mightest still the enemy and the avenger."

Yes, the Word is tight but it's right. I found out I would have to fight to keep that right. You have to believe, receive, and apply what you have learned. And most of all you have to spend time with God studying His Word. In 2 Timothy 2:15 it reads, "Study to shew thyself approved unto God, a workman that needeth not to be ashamed, rightly dividing the Word of Truth."

We have to tell the story, because Psalm 102:18 says, "This shall be written for the **generation** to come: and the people which shall be created shall praise the LORD." How will they know unless we tell them? Remember we are that new generation of **real people** who are not afraid to take a **stand for Jesus**!

You have to be fully persuaded that nothing can separate you from the love of God. We must apply and speak to whatever the situation using the Word of God with authority. Your victory is in your mouth—speak it! We are in a battle. Don't wait till it is over; shout now for you have the victory. If you are down for the count stand up and shout. To God be the glory, and I am going to tell His story!

Run a good race. Jeremiah 12:5 says, "If thou hast run with the footmen, and they have wearied thee, then how canst thou contend with horses? And if in the land of peace, wherein thou trustedst, they wearied thee, then how wilt thou do in the swelling of Jordan?"

Ask yourself this question: who or what is it that's causing me to fail? Galatians 5:7-8 says, "Ye did run well; who did hinder you that ye should not obey the truth? This persuasion cometh not of him that calleth you."

Conclusion: Victory

Whenever I get overwhelmed I always stand up. When I stand up it makes me feel like I am on top of any situation. Whatever the circumstance that's troubling me, it's under my feet! God has given us that authority. Psalm 8:3-6 reads, "Thou madest him to have dominion over the works of thy hands; thou hast put all things under his feet." Remember God said **greater works** shall we do!

Victory is **God's Spirit** inside of you!

Victory
In
Christ
To
Overcome
Real
You

Chapter Six

God's Word to Stand On

Romans 4:3-4 – For what if some did not believe? Shall their unbelief make the faith of God without effect? God forbid: yea, let God be true, but every man a liar; as it is written, that thou mightest be justified in thy sayings, and mightest overcome when thou art judged.

Romans 8:38-39 – I am persuaded, that neither death, nor life, nor angels, nor principalities, nor powers, nor things present, nor things to come, nor height, nor depth, nor any other creature, shall be able to separate us from the love of God, which is in Christ Jesus our Lord.

2 Timothy 2:10 – Therefore I endure all things for the elect's sakes that they may also obtain the salvation which is in Christ Jesus with eternal glory. He has already gone before us, to show us it could be done.

2 Timothy 1:13-14 – Hold fast the form of sound words, which thou hast heard of me, in faith and love which is in Christ Jesus. And that good thing which was committed unto thee keep by the Holy Ghost which dwelleth in us.

Revelation 22:16, 19 – I Jesus have sent mine angel to testify unto you these things in the churches. I am the root and the offspring of David, and the bright and morning star. And if any man shall take away from the words of the book of this prophecy, God shall take away his part out of the book of life, and out of the holy city, and from the things which are written in this book.

Revelation 22:12-13 – Behold, I come quickly; and my reward is with me, to give every man according as his work shall be. I am Alpha and Omega, the beginning and the end, the first and the last. And blessed are they that do his commandments that they may have right to the tree of life, and may enter in through the gates into the city. Your key is the Word of God.

1 Timothy 6:19 – Lay up in store for yourself a good foundation against the time to come, that they may lay hold on eternal life.

www.ingramcontent.com/pod-product-compliance
Ingram Content Group UK Ltd.
Pitfield, Milton Keynes, MK11 3LW, UK
UKHW041956230426
12048UKWH00008B/366